Original title:
Tales from the Tropicals

Copyright © 2025 Creative Arts Management OÜ
All rights reserved.

Author: Alexander Thornton
ISBN HARDBACK: 978-1-80581-802-1
ISBN PAPERBACK: 978-1-80581-329-3
ISBN EBOOK: 978-1-80581-802-1

Petals in the Breeze

A flower danced with a silly grin,
The wind told jokes as it twirled her in.
Bumblebees buzzed with laughter loud,
As petals swayed, a colorful crowd.

A cactus cracked a pun quite spry,
While palm trees waved beneath the sky.
The bloom said, 'I'm no wallflower here!'
And the sun winked, spreading good cheer.

The Spirit of the Tropical Sun

The sun wore shades, a funky sight,
Spreading rays with all its might.
It flashed a smile, a golden tease,
Sipping clouds like coconut freeze.

Bananas giggled from each tree,
As monkeys swung blissfully.
With every beam, a silly pun,
Who knew warmth could be this fun?

Reflections of a Sunset Tide

The waves whispered stories of fish in jest,
With jokes on the shore, they knew best.
A crab in a cape danced to a tune,
As the stars peeked out, making room.

Seagulls squabbled, competing for fries,
As the sunset painted the evening skies.
With each splash, a laugh echoed wide,
In this mirthful, magical, sunset tide.

Traces of the Hidden Waterfall

There's a waterfall hiding, so shy,
With splashes of laughter, oh my, oh my!
It tickles stones as it tumbles down,
Wearing a smile, not a frown.

Fish play peek-a-boo, a slippery game,
While frogs croak jokes, enjoying their fame.
In the mist, you can hear them all call,
'Join the party, at the waterfall!'

Whispers of the Island Breeze

The parrot squawks, a chatty tease,
While the palm trees sway with utmost ease.
A coconut drops, oh what a surprise,
Bumping my head, now that's no prize!

The sun beamed down, oh so bright,
Tan lines forming, what a sight!
But when I tried to take a dip,
A fish stole my flip-flop, that little chip!

Echoes of Coconut Dreams

Beneath the shade, I dream and doze,
While crabs march by in goofy rows.
A coconut falls, a crazy thud,
Turns out I'm just sitting on the mud!

A monkey swings with expert flair,
And steals my drink, without a care!
I chase him down, but he's too spry,
Now I'm left thirsty, oh me, oh my!

Sunlit Serenades in Paradise

With ukuleles strumming soft and sweet,
A turtle grooves to the tropical beat.
But watch your step, oh do take heed,
A spiky sea urchin is all you don't need!

As I sip my drink, a splash appears,
Not from the waves, but my friend's wild cheers.
With laughter loud and a playful shove,
We dance like fish, oh how we love!

Secrets of the Sapphire Shore

Shells and sea glass steal my gaze,
As I hunt for treasures in the sun's warm rays.
A crab holds court on a rock parade,
Judging my moves, unafraid!

The waves whisper gossip, so light and free,
While a seagull swoops down, squawking at me.
A flip-flop lost, a favor for fate,
Now beachcombing's fun, just you wait!

The Dance of the Kaleidoscope Fish

In the water, they swirl and spin,
A joyful splash, where fun begins.
They wiggle and jive, with silly flair,
Making bubbles float up in the air.

A purple one dances, a yellow takes flight,
Chatting with crabs in the soft moonlight.
With each flip and twist, they stir up some cheer,
Even the seaweed starts to appear!

Parables of the Palm Fronds

The palms sway gently, waving 'hello',
They gossip about us, but we never know.
A balmy breeze tickles each leafy crown,
While lizards lounge in their leafy gown.

With a rustle and giggle, they tease the sun,
Whispering secrets of laughter and fun.
Each frond a storyteller, wise and spry,
"Stay here forever, just give it a try!"

Burst of Color in the Twilight Sky

As day bids farewell, the colors pop,
A canvas of oranges, it's hard to stop.
Pink flamingos dance with a wink and a grin,
As stars start to twinkle, inviting within.

The sun slips away with a playful wink,
While dolphins leap high, nearing the brink.
The laughter of children echoes nearby,
In the arms of the dusk, their dreams fly high!

The Night's Embrace Around the Fire Pit

A circle of friends, with shadows so bright,
Roasting marshmallows, a delicious delight.
The crackle and pop, like stories unfold,
As sparks take a dance, both daring and bold.

With cackles of laughter, and goofy old tales,
The moon joins the fun, as it softly pales.
In the warmth of the fire, we spin and we twirl,
Underneath the stars, let the magic unfurl!

Bamboo Shadows at Dusk

Bamboo sways in gentle glee,
Whispers secrets to the sea.
Crickets dance in evening light,
Chasing shadows, taking flight.

Frogs wear hats, so full of pride,
While fireflies take a fun-filled ride.
Laughter echoes through the glade,
As sun and moon begin to fade.

Beneath the Mango Tree

Beneath the tree, we gather round,
Where the juiciest fruits are found.
Mangoes fall with thuds so grand,
It's a fruit fight we had not planned!

Laughter spills like juice on grass,
As sticky fingers try to pass.
The parrots squawk, they join the fray,
Announcing we were here to play.

Lullabies of the Lagoon

In the lagoon, the frogs croon,
Muddy tunes beneath the moon.
Turtles bob with sleepy heads,
Swimming dreams, no time for beds.

Fish flip up with sudden flair,
Splashing all without a care.
Crab a waltz, it too can prance,
Under stars, the water's dance.

Footprints in the Golden Sand

Footprints mark our playful race,
As we zigzag, leaving trace.
Seagulls swoop, what a sight!
Dancing shadows, pure delight.

A crab in shades looks very cool,
While we splash, we break the rule.
Laughter rings, the tide's our friend,
As the sun begins to send.

Twilight Conversations with the Sea

The sea waves whisper jokes so bright,
Seagulls cackle, taking flight.
Crabs crack wise with sideways strut,
While fish swim by, giving a tut.

Stars above are laughing too,
Splashing moonlight, a glowing hue.
Jellyfish giggle, a wobbly ballet,
While dolphins dance, come join the fray.

Shells tell stories of yesteryears,
With salty tears, and splashes of cheers.
A starfish winks, a fishy grin,
In this realm where silliness can begin.

So come on down, don't be shy,
The sea is ready, just give it a try.
With each wave, a chuckle, a sigh,
In twilight's glow, let laughter fly.

Canopy Conversations of the Night

Under leaves, the critters meet,
Squeaky bats share snacks and tweet.
A wise old owl with a feathered hat,
Sings a tune to a cheeky rat.

The raccoons play cards, what a sight,
While fireflies twinkle, oh what light!
A sloth strums softly on a tree branch,
As lizards laugh with a wiggly dance.

Monkeys swing with comedic flair,
Telling tales of their jungle affair.
A colorful frog croaks a tune,
Underneath the watchful moon.

In this leafy retreat, joy abounds,
As giggles echo, no bounds are found.
With whispers and chuckles, the night takes flight,
In the canopy's embrace, sheer delight.

Coral Serenade: A Love Story

In vibrant reefs, a clownfish pranced,
With a cheeky shrimp, they both danced.
Anemones swayed to their funny song,
As turtles chuckled, singing along.

A love struck duo, so silly and bright,
Swapping tales in the shimmering light.
While parrotfish painted with strokes of glee,
They giggle and wiggle under the sea.

From floating bubbles to seaweed romps,
They entertain sunfish with their silly chomp.
A hermit crab shouted, "You two are the best!"
"Join in the fun, forget the rest!"

Their love story's woven in coral and jest,
With laughter and joy, they're truly blessed.
In this watery world, full of delight,
Their laughter echoes from day until night.

Under the Banyan's Watchful Eyes

Beneath the banyan with roots so wise,
Critters gather, sharing surprise.
A mongoose cracks jokes, quite the wit,
While a lazy lizard takes a comfy sit.

A squirrel's pranks keep spirits high,
As fables swirl and the cicadas sigh.
Old tales twist with a funny touch,
In this shady nook that we love so much.

Fireflies twinkle, playing tag,
As the storytelling flows with a gag.
"Remember when?" an armadillo grins,
And laughter erupts, a chorus begins.

Under banyan's canopy, life is a play,
With silly moments that brighten the day.
The night hums softly, with joy always near,
In this funny realm, filled with cheer.

Vignettes from the Island Village

In the village, the rooster crows,
A dance begins, the island glows.
With laughter loud and rhythm sweet,
The locals move, it's quite a feat.

The market stalls, a colorful sight,
With fishing tales that last all night.
A cat steals fish, with stealth so sly,
As villagers laugh and shake their fry.

A coconut falls; it lands with a thud,
Neighbors jump back, then squish in the mud.
Children giggle, oh, what a place,
In this paradise, we find our space.

And when the sun sets, painters arrive,
With brush in hand, they come alive.
The colors splash like kids at play,
In this village, it's always a sunny day.

Echoes of the Sunset's Palette

As daylight fades, the sand gets warm,
The beach becomes our vibrant forum.
With flip-flops flapping, we strut and sway,
In a sunset's glow, we find our play.

A parrot squawks, a cheeky sort,
With jokes that fly, a comic sport.
He mimics us, a crafty bird,
His antics leave us quite disturbed!

The palm trees dance with the ocean's breeze,
Swinging their fronds as if to tease.
We join the scene, with laughter bright,
Dancing shadows in the fading light.

As stars appear, we gather near,
With stories tall and snacks to share.
In the island air, we chuckle and grin,
The sunset's magic, where giggles begin.

The Mermaid's Secret Shoreline

Down by the shore, where sea meets sand,
She combs her hair with a starfish hand.
A mermaid with dreams, so funny and sly,
She giggles at fishermen passing by.

With seaweed braids and a giggling tune,
She'll lure you in under the moon.
But beware, my friend, of her playful charm,
For she'll engage you without any harm!

In marvelous waves, the dolphins dance,
Inviting all with a gleeful prance.
With fishy jokes and silly flips,
They tickle the tide with playful quips.

And when the tide ebbs, watch your step,
For shells may hide where little crabs crept.
A splash, a laugh, as the tides rush in,
On this secret shore, the fun won't thin.

Grace of the Green Iguana

In the jungle green, the iguana lounges,
Stretching out, she poses in branches.
With her sun-kissed scales and eyes so sly,
She chuckles at folks who wander by.

A lizard king, with a lazy flair,
He basks away without a care.
Each tiny breeze makes him sway and wiggle,
As tourists snap photos; he grins, he giggles.

From branch to branch, he makes his leap,
In search of snacks, he's quite the creep.
With fruit in tow, he chows down bold,
This island life never gets old.

And when evening calls, in shadows cast,
The iguana rests, his day unsurpassed.
With laughter in the night, he'll snore away,
Dreaming of mischief on another day.

Enchantment under the Palm Canopy

Under palms, a party swirls,
Monkeys dance with twirls and swirls.
A parrot sings a silly song,
While tourists laugh and get it wrong.

Coconuts drop with a thud,
Hitting heads; oh what a dud!
Yet laughter echoes in the night,
As fireflies twinkle, oh what a sight!

A crab in flip-flops shuffles by,
With a wink and a cheeky sigh.
The beach is alive, with giggles and cheers,
As the moon whispers stories to our ears.

Sandcastles rise and then they fall,
As wave after wave gives it their all.
Here under palms, no worry, no care,
Just merriment, laughter, and salty air.

Rhythms of the Rainforest Heart

In a rainforest, where shadows play,
Frogs sing tunes that sway and sway.
A sloth on a branch gives a sleepy yawn,
While monkeys trade jokes from dusk till dawn.

A parrot squawks with a flair so bright,
Dancing to beats of the soft moonlight.
Trees whisper secrets of ages gone by,
As the rhythm of life makes spirits fly!

A jaguar prances, with a wink and a grin,
Dreaming of lunch, but not quite in.
The jungle bustles with giggles and coos,
As critters unite to share silly news.

Bubbles of laughter float in the air,
As toucans trade tales without a care.
In this vibrant world, where joy's apart,
The pulse of the jungle beats in heart.

The Coral Reef's Lament

Deep below, where colors gleam,
Fish frolic in an underwater dream.
A clown through anemones, giggles abound,
While turtles glide without a sound.

A starfish lost its way to the dance,
Hoping to find romance by chance.
But fish just swim past, too caught in the rush,
Leaving the starfish in a mad blush.

Shells gossip secrets from ocean floor,
As hermit crabs knock and adore.
"Oh, the currents bring confusion galore!"
Sighs the reef, longing for more.

Bubble-blowers in schools make a fuss,
In a sea of laughs, there's always a plus.
So here we linger in colorful cheer,
With creatures that tickle our hearts, oh dear!

Solstice in the Serpent's Embrace

In the shade on this summer's day,
A serpent stretches, finding its way.
With a wink to the sun, it plays like a pro,
As lizards join in an epic show.

Dance with the shadows, twirl with the light,
All creatures bask in this silly sight.
The snake throws a party, all friends come near,
Hissing in laughter as it sips on cold beer.

Frogs leap like champs on a lily pad stage,
With a hop and a slide, they engage.
"Hey, don't steal my spotlight!" one frog shouts loud,
While the serpent grins, feeling quite proud.

As fireflies start to twinkle and play,
The forest erupts in a dance till the day.
In this embrace of fun and delight,
The solstice shines bright in the coolness of night.

Watershed Dreams in a Covesong

In a cove where the coconuts sway,
Crabs dance the limbo, come what may.
Fishes giggle as they swim by,
Chasing their shadows under the sky.

A parrot yells, "What's the plan?"
While a turtle takes a nap in the sand.
Seashells listen to the gossiping waves,
While starfish giggle in their little caves.

The surf's up, and so is the sun,
Sandy flip-flops are a lot of fun!
The octopus juggles shells with glee,
Making a splash for all to see.

As day fades, a bonfire glows bright,
Singing soft tunes into the night.
Laughter echoes, the party's alive,
In this cove where the wild things thrive.

The Call of the Endless Horizon

Along the reef, where the seashells play,
Surfboards wander in a clumsy ballet.
A dolphin chuckles, with a flip and a dip,
While the seagulls gossip and have a quip.

Turtles in shades roam the sandy sward,
As the crabs practice their courtly sword.
The fish throw a party, with a wave and a splash,
Turning the ocean into a flashy bash.

A sunset paints the sky in hues,
While mermaids serenade with ocean blues.
The breeze carries laughter, so contagious and free,
As we all dance to the rhythm of the sea.

With each tide, stories of joy unfold,
Each wave a pun, each ripple bold.
What fun it is, along this bright shore,
To revel in laughter and want for no more!

Whispers of the Rainforest

In the jungle where the monkeys swing,
You can hear the parrot cheerfully sing.
A lizard in glasses reads a book,
While frogs in tuxedos do their look.

The vines are tangled; the sloths are slow,
But the ants are racing in a fast-paced show.
The jaguar laughs, he can't believe,
How the plants wear hats on Halloween eve!

Cicadas hum a rhythm, a playful tune,
While the butterflies dance under the moon.
Invisible spirits toss confetti with flair,
Celebrating life in the warm, thick air.

With each step, joy leaps in our tread,
In this haven of green, where dreams are fed.
The whispers of the forest keep the secrets, so tight,
Come laugh with the creatures in this magical light.

Echoes of the Caribbean Breeze

In the bay where the laughter flows free,
Palm trees sway like dancers at sea.
The sun wears sunglasses, feeling quite bright,
While crabs learn to salsa, what a sight!

A goat on a surfboard steals the show,
Splashing around, saying, "Let's go slow!"
With a coconut drink, we toast to the fun,
As the day drifts away, under the sun.

The breeze tickles whispers, secrets unfold,
As starfish share stories, both funny and bold.
The waves roll in with a giggle and roar,
Inviting us all to come dance on the shore.

As night drapes a blanket of stars overhead,
We laugh till we cry, no worries to dread.
In these echoes of joy, our spirits ignite,
In this Caribbean haven, everything feels right.

A Pristine Whisper of the Waves

The ocean's kiss was quite a tease,
It laughed and danced, and gave a breeze.
A seagull squawked, with flair and style,
As fish below swam in a pile.

The sun set low, a glowing tease,
It warmed my toes with playful ease.
Crabs marched past in tiny boots,
And waved at me with little hoots.

A dolphin jumped, and what a sight,
It flipped and flopped, with sheer delight.
I thought to join, but lost my hat,
And ended up in seaweed spat.

So if you hear a splash and yell,
Just know I'm here, I'm doing swell.
With ocean laughter all around,
In this wild dance, pure joy is found.

Floating Lanterns and Moonbeams

Under the stars, the lanterns float,
Wobbling gently like a boat.
A crab tried to steal one for a feast,
But it got lost, not quite a beast.

The moon peeked down, a cheeky grin,
"I've got the shine, let the fun begin!"
Fish in the deep began to prance,
A jellyfish joined, to enhance the dance.

I tossed a wish to the night so bright,
Instead got splashed by a dolphin's flight.
He chuckled loud, oh what a tease,
As I wiped water from my knees!

With laughter ringing through the air,
The ocean's party, beyond compare.
When dusk falls and lanterns gleam,
Just dive right in and live the dream.

The Quiet Elegance of Ocean Shells

I found a shell, so sweet and fine,
It whispered tales of the ocean's shine.
But wait! A hermit crab moved in,
And told me, "Buddy, this is my win!"

The shell said "hello" in such a squeak,
While the hermit crab danced, quite unique.
I couldn't help but laugh aloud,
As seaweed swayed, it looked so proud.

A starfish clapped; oh what a scene,
It glimmered bright in the sea's sheen.
"Join us for fun," the shells did say,
"Forget the day, just laugh and play!"

So in the sand, I made my throne,
With quirky friends, I felt at home.
The ocean's charm, it never fails,
A world of joy in all its trails.

A Canvas of Life Beneath the Waves

The ocean's brush, with colors bright,
Painted fish that danced in flight.
A sea turtle posing, oh so grand,
While a pufferfish made its stand.

Each coral reef, a work of art,
With laughter bubbling from the start.
An octopus pranked a passing seal,
With too many arms, it had great zeal.

The clams sang songs, their voices clear,
A bubbling rhythm, full of cheer.
A little shrimp, it joined the tune,
While others grooved beneath the moon.

So when you dive, don't hold back,
Join in the fun, find your own track.
In this grand canvas, spread your glee,
For beneath the waves, it's wild and free!

Colors of the Coral Kingdom

In waters where the fishes dance,
A parrotfish wears pants askew,
The sea anemone throws a glance,
At clownfish playing peekaboo.

Bright corals take a selfie show,
With octopus striking silly poses,
While starfish laugh at the flow,
Of waves that tickle their pink noses.

The turtles join with goofy grins,
And dolphins do their flip parade,
In this kingdom where fun begins,
Life's a splash, and never fade.

So come and see the colors bright,
In this realm where laughter thrives,
Where nature's full of pure delight,
And all the fish do high-fives!

The Heart of Tiki Tides

Beneath the shade of swaying palms,
A tiki mug spills coconut cream,
While crabs break into dance with calms,
Pinching shells, they form a team.

The tiki torches start to sway,
As laughter carries on the breeze,
A parrot sings a cabaret,
While monkeys dance up in the trees.

The waves keep clapping hands of foam,
As fishes pull off a grand show,
In this place we call our home,
Where mischief thrives and joy will flow.

So raise your cup and join the cheer,
With every sip, a giggle pried,
In the heart of tides, let's persevere,
In this nutty, tiki tide ride!

Whispers of the Sea Turtle

A wise old turtle speaks so low,
With tales of jellybeans afloat,
He claims to sail the sea, you know,
On crusty old bread with a coat.

His friends are fishes, bright and bold,
Who giggle at his fragile shell,
He says, "I've got a heart of gold!"
While riding waves, they cast their spell.

He wears a hat made out of kelp,
While seahorses nod, understanding,
Spinning stories, they laugh and yelp,
With every wave, their joy expanding.

So if you see him glide with glee,
Join in, don't let the fun subside,
For every laugh is a decree,
To cherish whispers from the tide!

Drifting Coconut Dreams

On sandy shores where coconuts roll,
Dreams float by on a gentle breeze,
Each one contains a secret goal,
And stories that will surely tease.

The crabs conspire to steal a bite,
While birds squawk nonsense from above,
The sun sets with colors so bright,
In this paradise, we find love.

As night falls, the coconuts sing,
Of tropical nights and starry beams,
With laughter echoing in a ring,
We drift away in our dream beams.

So let the waves lap at your feet,
Join in this wacky, playful scheme,
In every drift, there's joy so sweet,
As we share our coconut dreams!

Wind Chimes and Ocean Rhymes

Bamboo sways with secret jokes,
A pelican in shades just croaks.
The waves are laughing at the shore,
While crabs do a little jig and roar.

Seashells sing in salty air,
A kitefish tumbles without a care.
Those wind chimes dance with glee and cheer,
As coconut trees whisper bright and clear.

Flip-flops flapping with a beat,
Laughter echoes down the street.
A toucan's news from dawn till night,
Keeps spirits soaring, oh what a sight!

So join the fun, don't be late,
The ocean's party can't wait!
Grab a drink, enjoy the show,
Where every creature steals the glow.

A Hearty Welcome from the Gecko

On the wall, a gecko grins,
With tiny hands, he starts to spin.
He welcomes all who pass on by,
With a wink and a silly sigh.

"Stay awhile, don't rush away,
There's sun and bugs for here to play!
Join the ants, we'll dance in lines,
And sip on nectar from the vines."

In the evening glow, he brags,
About his skills at dodging jags.
With every twist, he winks and cheers,
"Life's too short, let's shed our fears!"

So if you're lost, just stop and see,
The gecko's call is wild and free.
He's got a smile for all to share,
And a cozy rock for you to spare.

The Cacao Tree's Whispers

In cocoa groves where secrets lay,
The tree hums sweetly all the day.
Chocolates dance upon the breeze,
While monkeys munch with cheery ease.

"Come try my treats!" the tree confides,
As critters gather in joyful tides.
Each nibble brings a chuckle loud,
As flavors burst, they feel so proud.

With beans of brown and whispers sweet,
The tree's delight is hard to beat.
A hiccup here, a giggle there,
With every bite, they're free from care.

So lift your cup to chocolate dreams,
In every sip, the laughter beams.
A world so warm with joy in taste,
Where frolic fuels our cocoa haste.

Legends Written in Sand

Footprints dance where the waves kiss,
A sandy stage for some beach bliss.
With every step, stories unfold,
Of crabs that dance and tales retold.

A starfish plays a game of tag,
While sea turtles tease with a brag.
"Who can float? Who can glide?
In this sandy realm, we all take pride!"

Castles rise from grains so neat,
With moats that surely can't be beat.
Shells are crowns, they rule the land,
Legends drawn by a sprinkle of sand.

So gather 'round under the sun,
Where every grain can be such fun.
With laughter echoing through the night,
These sandy tales feel just right.

Dance of the Fireflies at Twilight

In the warm dusk, they twinkle bright,
A swarm of giggles in flight.
Bumping into arms and legs,
These tiny lamps with buzzing pegs.

They flutter past with mischief's grace,
Daring you to join the chase.
With each spark, a shout or squeal,
Dancing light, oh what a deal!

Behind the bushes, whispers grow,
"Catch us if you think you know!"
But in the dark, they wiggle free,
Like slippery fish in a giggly sea.

"Oh look! A shadow!" one does scream,
They dart away, it's quite a theme.
We laugh and chase, we tumble, roll,
In the glowing night, we lose control!

A Journey through the Driftwood Grove

Through the grove, what do we spy?
A crab in slippers, oh my oh my!
He dances sideways, proud and slick,
His little moves, they do the trick.

The trees all chuckle, roots in a twist,
Who knew driftwood could dance like this?
A parrot laughing, feathers bright,
Says, "Join the party! It's pure delight!"

A turtle trundles with a grin,
His shell a disco, let the fun begin!
The waves chiming in with a playful tune,
While starfish clap beneath the moon.

We join the jam with cheerful hoots,
Even the seaweed shakes its roots!
Driftwood dreams in every glance,
In this wild grove, we all prance!

Secrets in the Surf's Embrace

The waves come in with a bubbling laugh,
Gossiping secrets from the sea's behalf.
A starfish whispers to a shell,
"What's the latest? Do tell, do tell!"

Jellyfish float with a graceful jig,
Under the sun, they dance so big.
A fish in a tuxedo struts past me,
In a finny ball, so fancy and free!

A crab with a crown makes a regal spree,
"Don't mind my claws, just follow me!"
With every splash, with every cheer,
The surf's embrace is fully here.

We laugh with the tide, counting our wins,
In the ocean's arms, everybody spins!
Secrets ripple with every wave,
In the surf, we find the brave!

The Hibiscus Blossom's Song

In the garden, blooms so bright,
A hibiscus sings, oh what a sight!
Its petals swirl in colors wild,
A floral dance, nature's child.

Buzzing bees come for a sip,
While butterflies take a joyful trip.
"Join us now for a bloom parade!"
They flutter around, lounge, and invade.

With a puff of wind, it starts to sway,
Telling the stories of the day.
"Oh here's a bee, oh there's a breeze,
Watch out for squirrels! They're such tease!"

A chorus of colors, a riot so bold,
The song in the garden never gets old.
In every petal, laughter sneaks,
The hibiscus knows, that joy it seeks!

The Rhythm of Rain and Roar

Pitter-patter on my roof,
A dance of droplets, far from aloof.
The frogs join in, a choir so spry,
While roosters hold auditions nearby.

Cows in the field, doing the jig,
Each splash of mud makes them big!
We're all left laughing, don't you see?
Rainy days spark pure glee!

Lizards skitter, tiny and quick,
Chasing tails, they do the trick.
A soggy ballet on the green grass,
With each leap, they make a splash!

Finally, the sun bursts through,
What will dry out? The mud or you?
The dance concludes, but never the fun,
In this wild world, we all are one!

Solstice in the Savannah

Under the sun, the lions lounge,
While cheeky monkeys plot to scrounge.
An ostrich struts, a flamboyant show,
With legs that go fast, and a head that won't know!

Giraffes peek down, curious and tall,
"What's new at the watering hole, y'all?"
The zebras crack jokes in black and white,
While hippos honk, oh what a sight!

The heat of the day makes everyone sigh,
But a parade of ants knows how to fly!
They've rigged up a boat from a leaf so green,
Rowing away to their underwater scene.

At dusk, the stars twinkle, laughter still loud,
With crickets chirping, they're all feeling proud.
In the savannah, chaos reigns sweet,
With each creature's pride, life's never discreet!

Legends Among the Lattice

In the garden where the vines entwine,
Tulips gossip, cross the fine line.
A snail tells tales, remarkably slow,
Of a race with the sun, how awful the glow!

Bees buzz around, with stories galore,
Of flowers that winked at them; oh, what a score!
The butterflies chuckle, sipping on dew,
"Those blooms are just tipsy, it's nothing new!"

A wise old tortoise, sitting so grand,
Claims he knows secrets from the great land.
But what do we hear? He snoozes instead,
While the blossoms lift petals, their joy widespread.

Amidst the laughter, the daisies sway,
With the breeze as their partner, they dance and play.
In this tangled abode, life's silly and bright,
Where even the weeds plot a hee-haw delight!

Sun-Drenched Farewells

As the sun dips low, it's time to say bye,
To the day's merriment, oh my, oh my!
Crickets audition, their evening song,
While the fireflies blink, "You've been here long!"

On the beach, the tide makes a fuss,
With seaweed snacks for the clam bus.
Seagulls squawk, claiming the last fry,
As children laugh, letting out a cry.

Palm trees sway, bidding farewell too,
With breezy giggles, a tropical cue.
A coconut tumbles, rolling down the sand,
While a dog chases shadows, it's all just grand!

With a wink of stars, the twilight begins,
The moon's in the pool, where laughter spins.
So here's to the night, let the good times swell,
In these sun-drenched evenings, all's well!

The Light Between the Leaves

Sunlight dances, playful and bright,
Lizards seem to bask in delight.
A parrot squawks, quite out of tune,
While monkeys plot mischief by noon.

Coconuts drop with a funny thud,
Splashing me right in the mud.
A breeze tickles the palm fronds high,
As I laugh at the clouds rolling by.

Bamboo flutes play a giggling song,
While crabs in the sand scuttle along.
Each leaf whispers secrets of cheer,
In this jungle, no room for fear.

A turtle moves at a leisure pace,
Dreaming of a dance-off race.
With each twist and turn, a funny sight,
Nature's jesters, oh what a delight!

Mirage of the Morning Mist

In the dawn, the waves start to glimmer,
A fish jumps out with a comical shimmer.
Coconuts floating, bobbing with glee,
Like little boats sailing to infinity.

Riddles of mist, swirling around,
A pipewrench crab groans without sound.
"Where's breakfast?" it seems to plea,
As dolphin giggles, "Try out the sea!"

The sun peeks through with a cheeky grin,
While gulls squawk out their morning din.
Turtles, puzzled, stare at the sky,
"Is that food up there?" they ask with a sigh.

Even the waves wave back at me,
In this dream, all is blissfully free.
Mirages playing tricks, how absurd,
But I can't help laughing at every word!

Islanders' Reverie

A hammock sways like a boat on the sea,
I swing and I giggle, so wild and free.
Fishermen weaving tales of scare,
While their catches happily float in the air.

The sunset spills colors, a vibrant mix,
As villagers gather for silly tricks.
Kites made of leaves take to flight,
While everyone dances, oh what a sight!

A dog chases shadows, a sight to behold,
While the islanders share stories retold.
"Did you see that?" a child squeaks with glee,
As a crab does the conga down by the sea.

Even the stars seem to twinkle and play,
As the moon joins in on the island display.
In this reverie, joy spreads like wine,
In the heart of the tropics, everything's fine!

Nectar of the Hibiscus

Hibiscus blooms in shocking pink,
I sip nectar, pause, and think.
Bees buzzing high with a 'dee-dee-dee',
I wonder if they want some of me!

Laughter is heard from the garden's side,
As frogs compete in a silly stride.
They croak a tune that's off the beat,
While I burst into laughter, can't stay on my feet.

Butterflies waltz with a flick of wing,
Spreading joy, oh what a thing!
I join the dance in this floral place,
With petals and pollen—a silly embrace.

The sun dips low, colors in a spin,
As creatures of whimsy join in the din.
Nectar's sweetness, laughter galore,
In this paradise, who could ask for more?

Nectar of the Tropical Flowers

In the garden where laughter blooms,
Bees gossip of sweet perfume,
Colors clash in a vibrant dance,
While a parrot tries its luck at romance.

The ants parade with tiny hats,
As a frog sings and the turtle chats,
Every petal, a tale to tease,
As butterflies flutter with such ease.

The sun shines down like a golden spoon,
Mangoes drop to a funky tune,
Lemons giggle, oranges wink,
While the coconut thinks, "I'm off to drink!"

In this patch of the silly and sweet,
Nature hosts a wild, cheerful treat,
With stories spun in every breeze,
And the creatures all aim to please.

The Tides Speak in Color

The ocean waves wear shades of blue,
While crabs dance in their bright red shoes,
Seashells whisper secrets of the tide,
And the fish giggle as they glide.

Dolphins leap with smirks so wide,
Each splash brings a tide of pride,
Jellyfish float with a wobbly glee,
While sea cucumbers just want to be free.

The sunset paints the sky a riot,
With colors so wild, you can't deny it,
Starfish wink, they've seen it all,
As the moon rises, some crabs crawl.

And in this watery laugh parade,
Every splash is like a charade,
Life's a joke in the sun and sea,
Where fun floats and everyone's free.

The Cargo of the Celestial Night

Stars twinkle like mischief on high,
Winking down with a twinkling eye,
The moon giggles, "Oh, what a sight!"
As wishes dance in the velvet night.

Clouds drift by with a cotton candy hue,
While comets race with a cheeky crew,
Fireflies twirl in a shiny show,
Creating designs that twinkle and glow.

Planets hum a curious tune,
As constellations sway in the light of the moon,
Each sparkle tells a story anew,
Of laughter and dreams that shine through.

So sit back and soak in the view,
As the cosmos plays hide and seek with you,
For in this universe, wild and bright,
Every moment is a delight in the night.

Odyssey of the Ocean's Bounty

The tides bring treasures, a feast for the eyes,
With squids doing jazz while the lobster cries,
Octopuses juggle with eight arms ablaze,
As the seaweed groans in a sea-sick daze.

Shipwrecks chat in a rusty old tone,
While dolphins ponder why they can't own a phone,
Crabs polish their shells, all shiny and neat,
As the starfish tap-dance with two left feet.

Bubbles laugh as they float to the sky,
Anemones play in their frilly tie-dye,
Seabirds swoop down, ready to munch,
On the buffet below, it's a seafood brunch.

So sail on through this watery spree,
Where laughter flows like the endless sea,
In this ocean of delight and cheer,
Every wave brings a giggle near.

The Journey of a Wayward Coconut

A coconut rolled, oh what a sight,
It danced down the beach all day and night.
With a wink and a twist, it met the sand,
Flirting with crabs, oh so grand!

In a game of tag, it hopped with glee,
"Catch me if you can!" it shouted, carefree.
But waves came rushing, wild and strong,
The coconut giggled, "This won't last long!"

It surfed the tides, a crazy ride,
Tossed by the sea, full of pride.
A dolphin laughed, "You think you're slick?"
But that coconut grinned, "I'm just a little quick!"

So here it goes, on adventures bold,
In this wild world, with stories untold.
Each splash and roll, with laughter wrapped tight,
A wayward coconut, full of delight!

Heartbeat of the Island

Beneath the palms, a drum did beat,
The island danced with joyful feet.
A parrot squawked, "Let's sing a tune!"
While a turtle crooned beneath the moon.

Each wave that crashed had its own song,
The rhythm of nature, where all belong.
From hibiscus flowers to the sandy floor,
Life's quirky melodies call for more!

A crab played maracas, quite confused,
While lizards jived, utterly amused.
"Come join our party!" the island proclaimed,
In this happy place, everyone's named!

So sway with the breeze, let laughter ignite,
Feel the heartbeat, soft and light.
On this joyful isle, where mischief meets cheer,
Every little critter holds fun tightly near!

Glassy Surfaces and Hidden Depths

A surface so calm, like a glossy sheet,
There's more to this water than just the heat.
Splash! A fish glimmered, quite a surprise,
"I'm hiding down here, just look with your eyes!"

Reflections of shells twinkled and played,
While a curious octopus silently swayed.
"Can you find me?" it asked, with a puff,
"Oh, what a game! Looks like it'll be tough!"

A bubble burst near a snail, quite strange,
"I swear I didn't do it, not my range!"
With a laugh, the sea stars just shrugged,
"This glassy surface has us all bugged!"

So dive in and treasure the secrets below,
Where laughter and quirks in tides freely flow.
From brightly spun corals to fish in a whirl,
In the island's embrace, it's a watery pearl!

Rituals of the Roaming Tide

As the tide rolls in, it carries a song,
A celebration of life, where all belong.
With starfish twirling and crabs at play,
Each wave brings whispers of a brand new day.

They gather on rocks, in a dash of cheer,
"A dance for the dawn!" they chime, "Let's hear!"
With funny little hops, they twist and twirl,
In this merry band, let laughter unfurl!

The seaweed sways, all green and bright,
"Don't forget us!" it laughs, "We love the night!"
So creatures unite, under the moon's glow,
In rituals of joy, the tides ebb and flow.

Through splashes and giggles, they share their delight,
Every roaming tide brings a whimsical night.
Nature's hilarity, so wild and free,
In the rhythm of waves, we find unity!

Secrets of Sunlit Canopies

Bright parrots squawk, gossip on leaves,
Monkeys swing by, pulling pranks with ease.
Coconuts drop, a surprise from above,
Nature's delight, oh, how we do love!

Lizards do yoga on sun-warmed rocks,
Bamboo shakes like it's dancing on socks.
The wind tells secrets in whispers so sweet,
While ants march in lines, never miss a beat.

Chattering frogs leap on lily pads wide,
Splashing in rhythm, taking all in stride.
Jungle's a party; come join in the fun,
With laughter and mischief, the day's just begun.

Sunset giggles as critters all yawn,
As day turns to night, the chuckles go on.
Under bright stars, with crickets in tune,
The wildest of nights is coming up soon!

Shadows on the Coral Reef

Fish in tuxedos, a vibrant parade,
Dancing with dolphins, a splashy charade.
Octopus skitters, a master of disguise,
While clowns in the sea wear their brightest ties.

Sea turtles do waltzes, taking it slow,
While shrimp spin around, putting on a show.
Coral plays host to a comical lot,
In this underwater jest, hilarity's caught.

The crab takes the stage with a sideways strut,
As jellyfish float like they're lost in a rut.
Manta rays glide in a graceful ballet,
In this reef of laughter, who needs to play?

Under moonbeams, the creatures unite,
For a twilight fiesta that's pure delight.
As shadows dance deep, and the ocean hums,
In the depths of the reef, humor always comes!

Nightfall in Paradise

Fireflies twinkle like stars playing peek,
As the night creeps in, the crickets all speak.
Mangoes are hanging like party balloons,
While coconuts giggle under bright moons.

The raccoons are scheming to steal the whole show,
Dancing in circles, putting on quite a glow.
Bananas wear smiles, swaying side to side,
In this tropical night, secrets can't hide.

The palm trees sway, tickled by soft breeze,
Whispering tales with a rustle of leaves.
Under the stars, all the parties collide,
In paradise's embrace, we laugh and we glide.

As the sun sets low with a golden grin,
The night bursts with laughter, let the fun begin!
In this whimsical world, where joy's our own path,
Every moment is gilded with whimsical math!

Storm Songs of the Tropics

Thunder rolls in like a cat with no shame,
The wind starts to howl, calling out all names.
Raindrops like marbles come thundering down,
As palm fronds shiver, removing their crown.

The coconut falls in a boisterous crash,
And frogs hop like they're in a mad dash.
With lightning as strobe lights, the dance floor's alive,
Nature's loud party, can you feel the vibe?

A pelican slides in, wearing a frown,
While the fish do a jig till skies turn brown.
In the tropical tempest, humor won't quit,
As thunderous giggles break free from the pit.

But once the storm's over and sun beams down bright,
The world laughs in colors, what a dazzling sight!
Oh, storms may be tempestuous, loud, and bold,
But in every rain dance, there's laughter to hold!

Secrets Beneath the Mango Tree

Lizards gossip in the sun,
While squirrels steal, just for fun.
Under the leaves, secrets flow,
Whispered tales that only they know.

A coconut falls with a loud thud,
Sending nearby ants into a flood.
Mangoes giggle, ripe and sweet,
As birds strut by, tapping their feet.

In the shadows where shadows dance,
A crab wears a hat, taking a chance.
The breeze tells jokes that twist and twine,
As children chase dreams with laughter divine.

Under the tree, the world spins round,
With every chuckle, joy is found.
Secrets bloom where stories meet,
Beneath the mango, life is sweet.

The Heartbeat of the Ocean

Waves tiptoe in with a splash and a dance,
Seagulls wear shades, taking a chance.
Crabs clap their claws in a rhythmic beat,
While fish gossip beneath the foam's heat.

A starfish poses like a superstar,
"Look at me! I'm not too far!"
The sun winks at the surf, so bright,
As dolphins prank, causing sheer delight.

Shells tell secrets in a bubbly murmur,
As seaweed sways, like a stylish firmer.
Every tide rolls in with a giggle and glee,
Beneath blue waves, life dances free.

The ocean teases with waves of cheer,
A slippery jellyfish appears near.
With every ripple, laughter flows,
The ocean's heartbeat, everyone knows.

Melodies of the Monsoon

Raindrops tap on roofs, a rhythmic song,
While frogs croak loudly, joining along.
The skies rumble, playfully tease,
As nature joins in with rustling leaves.

Puddles form with jump and splatter,
Kids splash wildly, as worries scatter.
Umbrellas spin like tops in a race,
Each one's bright, a smiling face.

Wind whispers secrets through branches high,
As lightning flickers, sparks in the sky.
The dance of monsoon, a jolly fate,
With every drop, a chance to celebrate.

So let the rain pour down like fun,
In nature's concert, we're never done.
With laughter woven in every tune,
Join the melody, under the moon.

Vines that Speak

Vines wiggle and squirm, gossiping loud,
About the flowers that piqued their crowd.
"Did you see that bee? He thinks he's so slick!"
They laugh as they twist, and dance, so quick.

A tree trunk joins in with a creaky laugh,
Swearing it's part of the comic staff.
The leaves rustle secrets, so bold and bright,
"Gossip's a game, let's play tonight!"

In the jungle, tales twist with ease,
Where every vine carries stories like these.
The wild whispers in a cacophony sweet,
Nature's humor, a warm-hearted beat.

From roots to tips, the laughter flows,
A symphony where every plant knows.
With every rustle, the day feels grand,
In this party of greens, come take a stand.

Tales of the Tidal Pool

In a tidal pool, where the crabs dance,
A fish tries to juggle, but loses its chance.
Starfish wear hats, posing for fun,
While seaweed plays tag, in the warm sunlight run.

The hermit crab grumbles, his shell's feeling tight,
As clams take a nap, dreaming of flight.
A jellyfish giggles, floats like a dream,
Silly things happen, or so it would seem.

A shrimp snaps a joke, making others all laugh,
While snails write their stories, each one a gaffe.
The tide comes and goes, with friendships so bold,
In this watery realm, their antics unfold.

With a flip and a splash, they end the grand show,
As the sun sets just right, casting evening's glow.
They wave their goodbyes, till the next tide renews,
In the tidal pool's laughter, there's always some news.

The Luna's Glow over the Bay

The moon winks down, casting silver on sea,
While seabirds perform, calling out, 'Look at me!'
A turtle in glasses scribbles his notes,
Counting the fish that he proudly promotes.

Crabs on the sand wear polka-dot ties,
While dolphins jump high, aiming for the skies.
The moon whispers secrets to waves soft and slow,
As shadows dance wildly in the warm evening glow.

An octopus dreams of a life on the stage,
Reciting old tales, turning a new page.
A parrot in pjs squawks songs of delight,
In the moon's cool embrace, all is merry tonight.

With laughter and giggles, the night drifts away,
As dawn peeks its head, turning night into day.
The moon takes a bow, bidding everyone cheer,
But promises to return, bringing magic each year.

Reflections in the Tropical Mirror

In a pond where the frogs wear glittery crowns,
And water lilies giggle, floating upside down.
A fish named Fred, with a flair for the bright,
Sings ballads to bugs, out of sheer delight.

The turtles hold contests, who can go slow,
While dragonflies judge, trying hard not to show.
A catfish with glasses is reading each line,
In the reflection of water, where everything's fine.

Up on the bank, a snake slips and slides,
Chasing the sun as it happily glides.
The trees burst with laughter as breezes come by,
Tickling the branches as the whispers fly high.

With splashes and croaks, the party rolls on,
In the mirror of life, there's never a yawn.
Each creature sings praises, their voices a cheer,
In this world of reflections, there's nothing to fear.

Symphony of the Singing Mangroves

In the mangroves swaying, a band starts to play,
With crickets on drums, and frogs leading the way.
The river laughs loudly, a giggling stream,
As turtles join in, fulfilling the dream.

The woodpecker's tapping a beat on the tree,
While otters bring snacks, shouting out, 'Yippee!'
Each branch makes a sound, a rustling encore,
In the symphony wild, they can't ask for more.

The wind chimes in with its breezy delight,
As fireflies twinkle, lighting up the night.
With melodies soaring, they fill the cool air,
Creating a concert, a magical fair.

As morning approaches, the music rings clear,
The creatures take bows, sharing smiles full of cheer.
In the mangroves' embrace, oh, what a night!
With laughter and song, everything feels right.

Hidden Echoes of the Rain

Puddles dance with smiles so wide,
The raindrops play, a slippery slide.
Frogs in tuxedos croak a tune,
As umbrellas twirl, they start to swoon.

A cat in boots, prancing with flair,
Dances around without a care.
Splashing through each little pool,
Making a splash, oh what a fool!

Beneath the trees, whispers abound,
Water sprites laugh as they rebound.
They tickle the frogs who leap and shout,
"Rain, rain, please don't leave us out!"

So when it pours, don't hide away,
Join the fun, let laughter play.
For in the rain, joy finds a way,
Echoing secrets, come what may.

Moonlit Paths on Sun-Kissed Sands

Under the moon's soft, glowing light,
Crabs in ballet pirouette with might.
A wise old turtle races the tide,
While seashells giggle, trying to hide.

Flip-flops squeak like a duck in glee,
As lovers stroll, counting stars they see.
A sudden wave gives them a splash,
"Oops!" they laugh, what a cheeky crash!

The palm trees sway in a dance of cheer,
Whispering secrets only they hear.
Sandcastles topple, what a delight,
As the moon winks, "Just stay in sight!"

So laugh with the night, enjoy the show,
For moonlit paths have a magical flow.
With each step taken, find joy to share,
On sun-kissed sands, without a care.

The Parrot's Vibrant Confessions

A parrot perched on a branch so bold,
Tells tales of pirates and treasures of gold.
With a squawk and a wiggle, he spins a yarn,
About a lost ship and a barnacle's charm.

Sipping on coconuts, he squints his eye,
"I once saw a crab that thought he could fly!"
With feathers bright, he struts and brags,
As curious lizards give him their tags.

"Did I tell you 'bout the fish in a hat?
He danced on a wave, imagine that!"
His laughter rings, a comical clout,
For every tall tale, he gives a shout.

So listen close, to what he means,
In a world where nothing's quite what it seems.
His vibrant confessions, a daily delight,
In a jungle where humor takes flight.

A Boat Ride through the Velvet Night

In a boat made of dreams, we glide and sway,
Through a universe where stars love to play.
A dolphin jumps, with a splash and a grin,
"Aren't we lucky, let the fun begin!"

The moon takes the helm, guiding our way,
As night creatures wave, "Hooray, hooray!"
A squawking parrot joins in the cheer,
"Let's race the waves, no room for fear!"

With laughter like bubbles, we float in time,
Fish in tuxedos begin to rhyme.
The night is alive with stories we share,
From seaweed singers to whimsical air.

So raise your cup, to this splendid ride,
In velvet night where dreams abide.
With each gentle wave, let joy take flight,
On a boat ride through hours of delight.

Enchanted Waters of the Silent Isle

In a lagoon where the fish wear hats,
A crab makes friends with jumping bats.
The turtles dance on their wobbly feet,
While octopuses twirl in a rhythmic beat.

A mermaid sings with a voice so sweet,
She tickles the whales, oh what a treat!
But watch out, dear friend, for the slippery floor,
That's where the sea cucumbers start to snore.

The dolphins giggle as they leap and bound,
Winking at seagulls that tumble around.
Anemones tickle the passing sun,
While the rays splash around, oh what fun!

So come take a dip in this whimsical bay,
Where laughter and splashes are part of the play.
Just don't be surprised if a fish makes a pun,
In the enchanted waters, the fun's never done.

Beneath the Canopy's Embrace

Where parrots squawk with a colorful flair,
And sloths debate who moves with more care.
The monkeys swing on their tangled vines,
Trading their snacks like secretive signs.

Under the leaves where the shadows dance,
A raccoon plots his next wild romance.
With berries and nuts, he lays down his feast,
Singing to creatures both furry and beast.

A chameleon changes to party attire,
As ants tell jokes, each one a live wire.
But beware of the frogs with their riddles to share,
They'll hops around while you sit in despair!

In this lively realm, where laughter takes flight,
You'll find all things joyful, a comedic delight.
So join in the fun beneath leafy climes,
Where the punchlines are plentiful, sprouting like limes.

The Drift of a Falling Feather

A feather floats down from a bird's great height,
Landing on a cat in a curious fright.
It jumps up and stares with its wide, goofy eyes,
While the feather just bounces, oh what a surprise!

The wind carries giggles from flower to tree,
As the feather does flips, wild and free.
Grasshoppers hop with a tap-dancing flair,
While the feather just winks, drifting through the air.

A parade of ants marches, forming a line,
They tiptoe around like it's all quite divine.
But the feather takes flight, soaring high and bright,
Leaving behind a cat that's dizzy with fright.

It twirls and it sways, such a comedic sight,
As it settles back down, bathed in soft light.
Who knew that a feather could cause such a stir?
In the world of the silly, life's always a blur.

Sonnet of the Starfish Dreams

Five-pointed wonders on the sandy shore,
They dream of adventures in ocean's galore.
With sun hats and sunglasses, they bask in the sun,
While giggling sea turtles join in the fun.

The starfish debate their favorite spots,
From coral castles to bubbly plots.
"I want to be a mermaid," one cries with a laugh,
While another wants to drive a jellyfish bath!

As crabs join the gossip, and seagulls squawk loud,
The starfish just lounge, feeling wonderfully proud.
"Forget about moving; we're perfect right here!
With laughter and bubbles, we've nothing to fear!"

So if you find five friends, soaking up beams,
Remember, dear friend, they're living their dreams.
In the salty embrace, with smiles that gleam,
These starfish remind us that life's but a dream.

Reverberations of an Island Beat

A parrot in a party hat,
Dances with a playful cat.
Coconuts roll down the street,
As the drums keep the island beat.

The fishermen all wear bright shoes,
And try to catch the dancing blues.
While island tides giggle and sway,
Fish shrug and swim the other way.

The old man sings a silly tune,
While chasing crabs beneath the moon.
The waves jump up, trying to rhyme,
With the rhythm of this island time.

Laughter echoes through the sand,
As tourists struggle to understand.
A local's joke, slight and sweet,
Turns the sun into a funny treat.

Heartstrings of the Wild Hibiscus

A hibiscus with a twinkling eye,
Laughs at bees that flit and fly.
With petals bright and stories bold,
It sways to secrets never told.

The garden gnomes hold tea in style,
With grins that stretch at least a mile.
They brag about their closest friends,
The frogs that croak and never end.

A breeze tickles leaves, starts a game,
Where twigs and branches take the blame.
A snail snickers, slow and sly,
As birdies chase the clouds up high.

In this paradise, life takes a twist,
Laughter louder than any mist.
Each flower's dance, a fun parade,
In a world where joy won't fade.

Longing from the Seaside Hammock

In a hammock strung near the coast,
A lazy man is quite a host.
He dreams of fish that wear a tie,
And seagulls singing lullabies.

With sand between his toes so fine,
He paints bold fish with a beachy line.
While sunbathers roll like kites in flight,
And stray dogs howl to the moonlight.

A crab slips by in a tiny waltz,
While tourists laugh without a halt.
A jumpy frog joins in the spree,
And asks if he can take a knee.

Dreams drift on the ocean breeze,
That's tangled up in swaying trees.
A giggling wave bursts with a cheer,
A serenade for all who hear.

Adventures in the Treetop Canopy

In the canopy where monkeys swing,
A squirrel wears a shiny ring.
With acorns dropped like clanging bells,
They mix and mingle with odd smells.

Chirps and chortles fill the air,
While butterflies do pirouettes fair.
A sloth attempts to start a race,
But naps defeat him in the chase.

Leaves converse in shilly-shally,
As lizards join in on the rally.
They giggle at the owls that stare,
With wisdom locked away in hair.

Adventures burst from trunks so wide,
Where creatures laugh and take great pride.
Each branch a tale of fun and cheer,
In this jungle, joy is near.

www.ingramcontent.com/pod-product-compliance
Lightning Source LLC
Chambersburg PA
CBHW070317120526
44590CB00017B/2718